DISCOVER
The Underground Railroad

by Margaret McNamara

Table of Contents

Introduction	2
Chapter 1 Who Were Slaves?	4
Chapter 2 What Did the Underground Railroad Have?	10
Chapter 3 Why Was the Underground Railroad Important?	14
Conclusion	18
Concept Map	20
Glossary	22
Index	24

Introduction

The South had **slaves**. The slaves had the **Underground Railroad**.

It's a Fact
Slaves were people. Other people owned slaves.

Words to Know

 escape

 freedom

 plantations

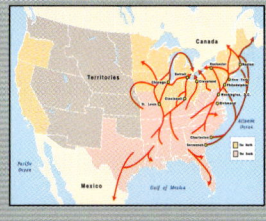 routes

 slaves

 Underground Railroad

See the Glossary on page 22.

Chapter 1

Who Were Slaves?

Slaves were people.

▲ Slaves were not free people.

Slaves were people in the South.

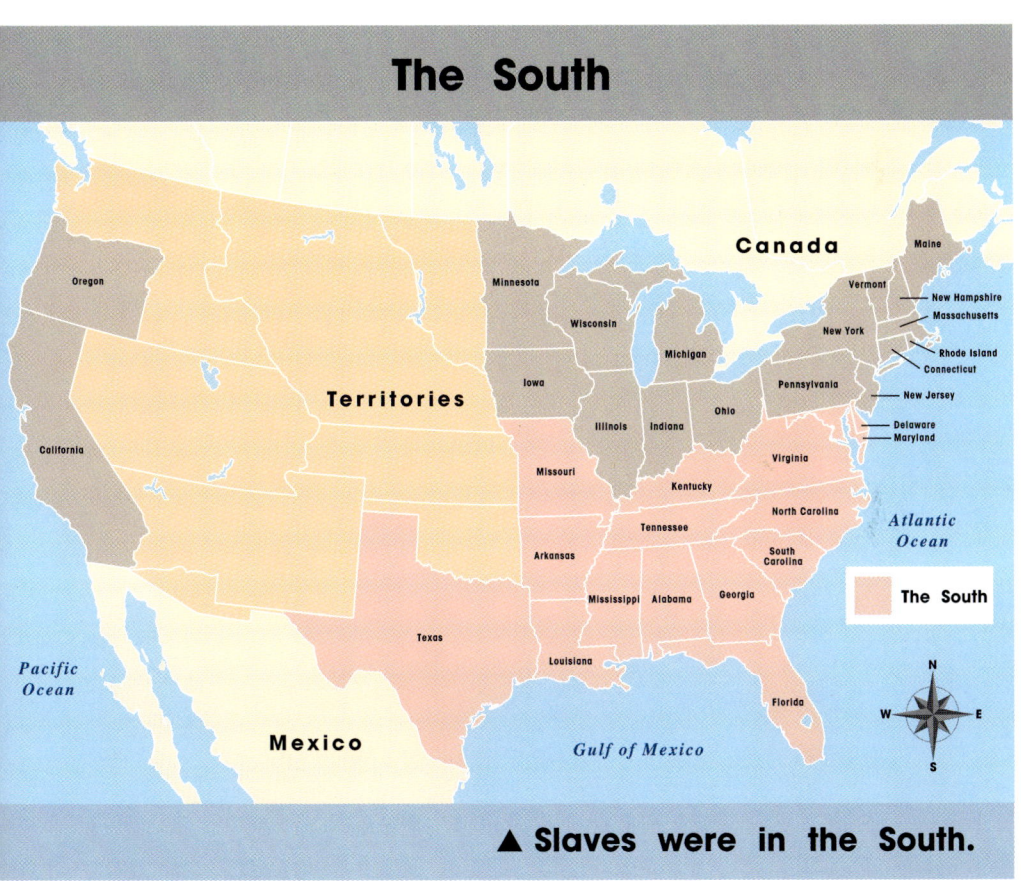

▲ Slaves were in the South.

Chapter 1

Slaves were workers.

▲ Slaves were workers in the South.

It's a Fact
The South had slaves. The Civil War started. Then the slaves were free.

Who Were Slaves?

Slaves were workers on **plantations**.

▲ Slaves were on plantations.

Chapter 1

Slaves were workers in fields.

▲ Slaves were in fields.

Who Were Slaves?

Slaves were workers in mills.

Did You Know?
Mills change cotton. People use cotton from mills.

▲ Slaves were in mills.

Chapter 2

What Did the Underground Railroad Have?

The Underground Railroad had **routes**.

It's a Fact
Many slaves followed the routes.

Pacific Ocean

The Underground Railroad had routes to the North.

The Underground Railroad had routes to Canada.

The Underground Railroad had routes to Mexico.

The Underground Railroad

▲ The Underground Railroad was routes.

Chapter 2

The Underground Railroad had people.

▲ The Underground Railroad was people.

What Did the Underground Railroad Have?

The Underground Railroad had houses.

▲ The Underground Railroad was houses.

Did You Know?
The Underground Railroad was not a railroad.
The Underground Railroad was not underground.

Chapter 3

Why Was the Underground Railroad Important?

Slaves used the Underground Railroad.

▲ Many slaves wanted the Underground Railroad.

Slaves used the Underground Railroad to **escape**.

▲ Many slaves wanted to go North.

Did You Know?
The Underground Railroad was before the Civil War.

Chapter 3

Slaves used the Underground Railroad at night.

▲ The slaves wanted to escape.

Why Was the Underground Railroad Important?

Slaves used the Underground Railroad for **freedom**.

▲ The slaves wanted freedom.

Conclusion

Slaves used the Underground Railroad. Slaves used the Underground Railroad for freedom.

Concept Map

The Underground Railroad

Who Were Slaves?

- people
- people in the South
- workers
- workers on plantations
- workers in fields
- workers in mills

What Did the Underground Railroad Have?

- routes
- people
- houses

**Why Was
the Underground
Railroad Important?**

slaves escaped

slaves had freedom

Glossary

escape get away

*Slaves used the Underground Railroad to **escape**.*

freedom to say and do what you want

*Slaves used the Underground Railroad for **freedom**.*

plantations big farms

*Slaves were workers on **plantations**.*

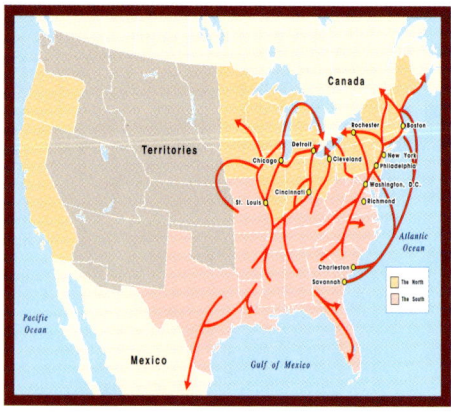

routes ways to follow

*The Underground Railroad had **routes**.*

slaves people owned by other people

Slaves were workers.

Underground Railroad (1) routes slaves used to escape; (2) the people who helped slaves escape

The slaves had the Underground Railroad.

Index

Canada, 11

escape, 15

fields, 8

freedom, 17-18

houses, 13

Mexico, 11

mills, 9

North, the, 11

people, 4-5, 12

plantations, 7

routes, 10-11

slaves, 2, 4-9, 14-18

South, the, 2, 5

Underground Railroad, 2, 10-18

workers, 6-9